IT IS IN THE BLOOD

The old saying "It's in your blood accurately describes my two oldest children Zach and Melinda. Both well-educated and highly paid Lawyer & I T Sales Manager.

They started in car business as teenagers. Melinda sold her first car at 15. Zach worked in Auto Retail, Auto Wholesale and Automotive Finance before he was 21. Both can sell cars today as good as any Auto Sales Professional.

IT IS IN THEIR BLOOD

Do What You Love
&
Love What You Do

That is the perfect way for you to always enjoy your work, always be good at your work, always be the highest paid at your work and always be happy at your work

Take Less Ups - Sell More Cars
It Aint Rocket Science

Take Less Ups, Sell More Cars—

"It Aint Rocket Science"

"Johnny Mack" Jones

It is simple to sell lots of cars

Testimonials

What are others saying about this Johnny Mack?

"I watched Johnny Mack live this book on the wholesale side of the automobile business. A must read for everyone in the car business"

    Neal Carter   General Manager   Auto Auction

I have spent my entire career in the car business. I wish I had read this book on my first day.

    Mike Smith, Dallas, Texas

Johnny Mack was the best sales manager I ever worked for. I had worked at selling cars for 6 months when he was brought in as sales manager. I had heard he was different and quick to fire a salesman if they messed up, but his management style was just the opposite. He was positive, encouraging and helped me become a highly productive member of the sales force. I am a sales manager myself at a Chevrolet dealer in California now. I make a great living and enjoy running my 15-man sales crew. I try to act just like Johnny Mack acted when I work for him.

Frank Roberts Los Angeles, Ca

Take Less Ups - Sell More Cars
It ain't Rocket Science

"Johnny Mack" Jones

Horse Sense Publishing
P.O. Box 1317
Fayetteville, Tennessee 37334

Title: Take Less Ups, Sell More Cars—It ain't Rocket Science

Author: Johnny Mack Jones

Editor: Aron Jones

Publisher:
Horse Sense Publishing
PO Box 1317
Fayetteville, Tennessee 37334

All rights reserved. Any reproduction or transmission, in any form or by any means, electronic or mechanical, including but not limited to photocopying, recording, or by any information storage and retrieval system, without written permission from the publisher, is prohibited.

Copyright © 2019 by Horse Sense Publishing First Edition 2019
Published in the United States of America

Dedicated to

All the honest, hard-working salesmen who love and believe in what they sell and want to sell more

Table of Contents

Forward

The Secret Sauce

A License to Print Money

Becoming a "Shopper Stopper"

Understand Your Customer

Know What You Are Selling

Have a Good Attitude

Overcoming Car Salesman's Bad Rap

Summary

My Favorite True Story

Foreword

I have never worked a day in my life without selling. If I believe in something, I sell it, and sell it hard.

—Estée Lauder

As a kid I never dreamed of being a fireman, policeman, or politician. I never dreamed of being a doctor, lawyer, or astronaut. I have, from my earliest days, dreamed that I would make my living selling cars and trucks. In 1973, at 17 years old, I got my chance. Within three hours I sold my first car.

Many colleagues of mine over the years have called me one of the best car salesmen they have worked with. Am I? I do not know—or care. What I do know, however, is I have always worked as hard as any other salesman I had the pleasure of working alongside. And along the way, I learned a thing or two about selling cars.

This book is my way of sharing what I learned over the last forty-plus years. It is also my way of responding to a growing frustration of mine; a frustration of watching other salespeople mess up the remarkably simple things necessary to sell more cars—without burning through the ups. Dealerships go to great lengths to get potential customers on the phone, to their website, and on the lot. Burning through those customers is, therefore, not a sign of good salesmanship, it is a sign of wasted effort.

Here is what my years of experience have taught me. Customers call, click, and visit dealerships to get answers to a few critical questions. Questions they cannot get answered on their own:

Why buy *this car*?   Why buy at *this dealership*?

Why buy from *this salesperson*?   Why buy *now*?

This car, this dealership, this salesperson, right now. That is what a good salesperson always has at the forefront of every communication with a customer.

In writing this book—with the assistance of my editor—I desire to teach rookie salespeople an easy, fun way to get the basics right—how they can take less ups, sell more cars. I also want to give more seasoned salespeople a chance to step back and reflect on experiences that they will have shared with me. In doing so, I hope that my perspective will be like a collaboration that leads them to improve their technique and, ultimately, become more effective. In the end, this book aims to help all salespeople do more with less; to take less ups and sell more cars. It is not rocket science.

This book comes from the heart. I know it sounds corny, but I love people and I love cars. I have greatly enjoyed my career in the car business. I got to spend my career with people talking about cars. It has truly been fun. Getting paid for having fun? What a life I have lived! As I no longer have the simple pleasure of doing that daily, this book is my way to relive and enjoy again the many truths I learned from my many friends and customers I had he pleasure of working with, and for, over the years. Some of whom I suspect will enjoy reliving their story as well.

INTRODUCTION

The Secret Sauce

Fact is, there really is a secret to taking less ups and selling more cars. Like most secrets, however, it turns out to be simple. As you will glean from the stories I use to teach my system, I am not well educated, or especially intelligent. I am a country boy from the backwaters of the Mississippi Delta. When I tell you it ain't rocket science, you can take that to the bank.

The real secret is an understanding of people. Do you want to sell more cars? Understand what your customers want. Do you want to do it without burning through leads? Have a plan. Having the gift of gab, as they say, will only get you so far. Once you understand what your customers want, you just must develop a system that responds to those wants. Like anything else in life, being purposeful—having a plan—is critical.

However, plans are only as effective as the discipline with which those plans are executed. If you want to be successful, you must consistently follow the plan. The most important step is to use the system every day, with every customer. No exceptions. If you want the system to work, you must feed that system.

The System works if

you work the System

That really is all there is to it. Too simple? I told you it was. Of course, what I just described begs the question the rest of this book seeks to answer.
In practice, my system is just like any other: It is all about consistency. It is about developing good habits. About limiting bad habits. Most importantly, it is about following a system designed to meet the needs of your customers. If you do, you will develop the remarkable habit of taking less ups and selling more cars. And what a habit that can be.

I am often asked, "who is this program is designed for? Is it for me?" My response is the same: it is designed for those that want to be the best and highest-paid salespeople in America. Is that you? If so, keep reading, this is a book for you.
Truth is, I could—and almost did—call it "The Lazy Salesman System" because it really requires less effort than most of the sales systems used today. It is not complicated. It truly is designed for the lazy salespeople who want to succeed—sounds too easy, right?

Before we get into the nitty-gritty, let me go ahead and address the cynics reading this—you know who you are. Every time I talk to a group of salespeople, there is always at least one person who takes upon him or herself the responsibility of deciding my system would never work or that his or her own way of doing things is far better. And you know what, it might be. But I will put my numbers, year in and year out, against the best in the business.

Often, the know-it-all who feels compelled to point out why this system would never work is typically an underachiever. Cynical salespeople tend to consistently perform poorly, regardless of how many years' experience that may (or may not) have. They also seem to always have a system that works better than mine. To all these naysayers and negative folks out there, I tell you this:

If you hate where you work or what you do, quit; even if you are making good money, quit. You will become more miserable as time goes on. And you are a cancer affecting everybody around you. Do yourself and the car lot a favor and quit right now.

For those with a system that works better than mine, great! Use it! There is no such thing as a universal system that is perfect for everyone. There is also no such thing as a perfect system. I bet that if you read this book and are honest with yourself, there is something you can learn and add to your system to make it better. And if you can take a suggestion, or two, from this book and add it to your system, I will have accomplished my goal.

Years ago, I worked for a consulting company installing sales systems at dealerships across the country. I learned salespeople, almost universally, believe the sure-fire way to increase sales is to increase traffic on the lot. Salespeople especially want more foot traffic. More leads. More customers. More ups.

There was, and is, a fundamental belief among salespeople that the best explanation for poor sales numbers is poor traffic. Not enough leads. Not enough customers. Too few ups. There can certainly be some truth to that, especially in the extreme.

The relationship between foot traffic and sales is, however, vastly overstated. I recall a question I was once asked by a young salesman at an engagement in Missouri: "How do you plan to increase sales here; are you going to start doing lots of advertising?" My answer: "If you're waiting for the rush to come, it is not coming. I'm not here to bring you more ups, I'm here to help you do more with the ups you are already getting."

If You Are Waiting for the Rush ... It is not Coming
The inherent belief that a young salesman in Missouri had twenty years ago is still held by many salespeople today. The answer today is even more true than it was twenty years ago.

Increasing sales by increasing foot traffic are the most costly, inefficient, and silly way to increase sales. Think about it. Getting customers on the lot is awfully expensive. It requires advertising, marketing, promotions. All of which cost the dealership a lot of money. Then, once the customer is on the lot, they are there to capitalize on whatever sale, discount, or other gimmick used in the advertising, marketing, or promotion. So, customers obtained this way comes with a lot of costs.

The cost incurred to get a customer to the car lot and convinced to buy is called the Customer Acquisition Cost (CAC). In the car business, the marginal cost to increase foot traffic has the highest CAC of any other lead. Said differently, the cost to drive foot traffic above what a lot normally gets based on its location, referrals, and other inherent factors have the highest cost. Once that customer is on the lot, the dealership is in the hole and the only way to break-even is to turn that shopper into a buyer—to make a sale.

High CAC has a direct impact on the salespeople, not just the dealership. There are only so many ways to slice a dollar. As CAC rises, less profit is available to compensate the person making the sale. Whether pure commission, base plus commission, per unit, or pure salary; if the dealership is spending more money to create-ups, there is less money to compensate the salespeople. There are only so many ways to slice a dollar. Therefore, maximizing profit (including minimizing CAC) has a direct impact on the individual's salesperson's bottom line. Do I have your attention yet?

I have skills learned over four decades. My skills were not something I learned in school. I learned them through trial and, yes, error. They are not difficult and may seem overly simplistic. But I am confident that if you read and apply them, they will improve your ability to turn-ups into sales. And to do so at a high rate.

The rate with which you turn an up into a deal is what I refer to as your closing ratio or rate. For example, if you take five ups per day and average one deal out of those ups, you have a closing ratio of 1 to 5, or 20%. In my experience, a great salesperson will close around 20% of foot traffic. A less efficient salesperson will be closer to 1 to 20, or 5%.

Now let me show you an example of why these matters. Let me use an example of a dealership that needs to generate $40,000 in gross margin per month to meet the budget. Let's also assume that on average, this dealership averages $2,000 in gross margin per car sold. That means the dealer needs to sell 20 cars per month. If that dealer spends $10,000 per month on generating ups, the CAC is $500—which is on the good side of average. However, what this calculation misses—and what most advertising and marketing folks will not tell you—is the potential impact of better salesmanship.

In that same example, if the sales force is closing 10% of all ups—foot traffic, phone calls, and internet leads—the cost per up is $50. In other words, their sales force is "touching" 200 potential customers per month and letting 180 slips through their fingers. What if that dealership increased the close rate by only 5%; what if they closed 15% of their ups?

Now that dealer would only need to bring in 133 customers. Assuming the marketing department is equally as efficient with its efforts to generate ups, the dealer in our example has lowered its CAC to just $332.50. A 5% increase in the close rate lowered the CAC by more than 66%!

Dealers who realize this do not lower their marketing. What they do—because of the increased return on investment (ROI)—is continuing to bring in 200 customers per month. By doing so, the dealer sells 30 cars instead of 20. And increases the gross profit from $40,000 per month to $60,000. Who gets those extra 10 deals a month? The salespeople are now closing as they should. And I promise you the dealer will be happy to write you a bigger check at the end of each month.

This book is not a marketing book. It is also not a management book. It will not teach you how to appraise a trade-in. And it will not teach you how to sell in the service lane—those books are in the works. It is a book about selling cars as efficiently as possible.

What follows is an uncomplicated set of guidelines. Guidelines that work. I encourage the seasoned salespeople to mix these guidelines into their approach to waiting on customers every day. Use them with every up, every time, with no exceptions, and the results will be an amazing increase in your productivity. You will see your close rate increase. Implemented dealership wide, these simple guidelines will lower CAC.
The system is a thought process, a mental checklist, if you will, that leads to controlling the flow of your deals.

Be methodical and calculated. I have always been a strong closer because I am purposeful with my plan. Every move must be intentional. Every question must yield the desired answer. Every step must be one step closer to delivery.

Wasted steps, unthoughtful questions, and pointless conversation not focused on answering the questions your customer needs to know is an inefficiency great salespeople avoid.

How is as important as *what*. Everything a salesperson does involves both substance and procedure; a what and how. Without fail, salespeople should be enthusiastic, polite, and respectful. Kindness goes a long way. Who wants to buy a car from a jerk?

Ask the right questions.

Asking the right question is only half the battle; you must ask it correctly. Showing the right car, the wrong way will lose a deal. Answering a question correctly is wrong if done wrong.
If you put the work in to get the *what* right, do not let the *how* kill your sale.

To get the *what* right you must listen. Many salespeople ask a question only to get the customer to give an answer the salesperson wants. For example, they might ask if the customer trades their vehicles every two or three years?
The intent of this question is probably to allow the salesperson to discuss the virtues of a lease. Or a feeble attempt to "lead" the customer.

"This car will work for you, right?"

Nothing wrong with that, right. Wrong.

If a person has been trading their car every two or three years over the last decade, I assure you, they know about leases. They do not need you to "take" control of them. And they also know what a pushy salesperson is—and how to ditch them.

xvi

The real reason why these types of questions are wrong is because by the time such a question is appropriate, the salesperson should already know whether the customer trades their car every two or three years.

How? By listening to their customer. A lease is a finance option and not a question a salesperson should typically be asking until they already know the information. I ask a question then LISTEN. Closely. I want to get information that will help me toward delivery. I want to help; and I believe most customers want my help.

I have helped customers buy a VW Beetle that first asked if we had any 4x4 diesel trucks and vice versa.
I have seen parents ask for something around $5000 for a college kid that drove out with a brand-new car. How do you get this kind of results on a regular basis? It is simple.
The Power of listening and suggestion makes it happen.

I certainly did not get those results by asking closed-ended questions; by pushing finance options before the product being financed; and I did not get those results by being pushy. Why did they say they were looking for a $5000 car? My thinking when I heard these requests were: (1) is that how much they must spend or (2) is that what they think will get their payment where they want it.

But the time to ask those questions is not in the first few minutes. I log that information in my mind and continue to gather information—while we walk over to the $5,000 cars. At this point, you should already know you have a deal.
This is just a matter of selling the right car.

My system is not designed to burn through these kinds of ups in search of a laydown. It is designed to sell customers the right car for their needs, at a fair price they will be happy to pay.

My system is designed to give you better close rates, happier customers, and increased repeat and referral business. Listening is critical to my process.

I'm going to take this example another step further. If the customer above is under the impression that a car for this amount has a payment of $250 a month then I have several suggestions to make. However, first, I am going to show the customer exactly what they asked for.

Once they see that the amount, they have asked for will not get the car they envisioned, now I can begin to suggest other options. If they react to the cheaper car by commenting on how old it is, the number of miles, or the lack of features which newer cars have I might suggest that the payment they want may work on a newer, economy car; the warranty removes the risk that miles carry; and even today's economy cars have many bells and whistles. And by buying new, the payments can generally be spread out over a longer period, thereby reducing the payment.

Simple suggestions like my example above are easy moves that really do make sense. Moreover, most people will like your suggestion. The point is that it is all about the basic sales skills of introduction; about being kind and helpful; about visiting with your customer to slow them down enough to try all your evolving options until you get the one that will work. Then finish the delivery. Have you learned anything yet? Well, this is just the introduction. Understanding my guidelines will help you become a better salesperson; it will make you ready to

Take Less Ups Sell and More Cars

It Aint Rocket Science

Good Time Management

"Time Spent with A Customer

Is Time Well Spent"

"It's Cheaper to keep a Customer

than find new one"

The longer you are with an up the higher probability of closing the sale. If you have a unit on the lot up will buy, then that is where your focus should be. Find out what are the obstacles to closing on it then use your time to do whatever that is. Therefore, just visiting about any and everything with the up becomes an important tool to slowing them down and getting the answer to what obstacles stand in the way.

An example would be customer cannot buy without spouse, cosigner etc. then get in unit with customer and go see whoever can help you close the deal. You must pull out all stops to remove all obstacles. Every minute of your workday not with customer must be geared towards prospecting or follow-up. Spending more time with up reduces the number of follow up phone calls daily reduce paperwork and calls.

Many Times

    The Things You

        Failed to do

           Made the Other

                Dealership's

                    Salesperson's Job

                        A Lot Easier

                            Never Give Up

Chapter 1

Taking Less Ups Is [Still] a License to Print Money

Things have changed since my days as a salesman walking the lot. In the 1970s and 1980s, customers had much less information than they do today. Even into the 1990s, as the information age began to blossom, extremely limited information, by today's standards, was available to the everyday customer. Accordingly, salespeople held a large informational advantage—an advantage that was all too often misused by salespeople. That opportunistic behavior led to a bad reputation for salespeople in the car business.

Today's Customers are Ready to Buy

Today's customers are quite different. They are well informed; so too must the salesperson be well informed. The bad news is car lots will seldom look like Times Square on New Year's Eve. The good news is that it does not matter.

Today's customers are much, much closer to making a buying decision when they do show up on the lot or make the phone call. They do not come to the lot looking for information they cannot get elsewhere. Instead, they come to the lot after they have much of the information they got from salespeople in the past. They come to the lot ready to buy.

In the 1970s, most customers came to the car lot to get information. Now they go to Google. In the 1970s, customers came to the car lot to see the new models. Now they go to Google. In the 1970s customers came to the car lot to get the price of a car.

Now they go to Google—and they do not only get the price, but they get what the dealer paid for it! Salespeople must be aware of this fact. While you cannot assume all the information, they have is correct, you must assume they are informed.

Today's customers are buyers. Think about it. The only good reason for a customer to be at the lot—or on the phone—is because they want to buy. The only reason they would email you is to buy. The only reason to instant message you are because they want to buy. By the time, a salesperson has contact with a customer; the customer is beyond just looking for basic information. They got all the basic information they wanted from Google. They contacted you because they are ready to buy. So, what is left for the salesperson to do?

Today's customers are looking for salespeople to answer some quite simple questions; questions google cannot answer. Most salespeople, however, spend extraordinarily little, if any, time addressing these questions.

What customers want to know is:
Why buy *this* car?
Why buy at *this dealership*?
Why buy from *this salesperson*?
And why buy it *now*?

Everything I say and all the information I give to a customer must answer one of these questions. Anything else is wasted. That is what customers want from their salesperson, even if they do not come out and ask.

As a consultant, the answers I gave to salespeople of yesterday are the same as I give to salespeople today. Despite all the changes in the business, and they are vast, people have not changed. They are the same. In many ways, the job of selling cars today is even easier because the information age has made customers more informed and ready to buy on their first contact with a salesperson. The bottom line is it is easy to teach salespeople to sell more cars with less ups—to be more efficient. The skillset salespeople today need is the same as they needed in years past. Great salespeople today do what great salespeople have always done:

Close a higher percentage of ups

Increase repeat and referral business

Lose fewer deal

Package deals so they can be approved.

Stop customers from backing out

Find easy deals Salesmen walk past

These and many more are the skills that lead to selling more cars without burning through ups. And the genuinely interesting thing is more ups will not help you develop these skills.
The answer is not more ups, it is a better system.

Top salespeople do not take twice as many ups as the next closest salesperson. Salespeople who take more ups than anyone else are not a dealership's top salespeople. Those salespeople are the dealership's most expensive salespeople; most inefficient salespeople; and least desirable salespeople.

Salespeople who burn through ups cost the dealership—and every other member of the sales crew—far more money than they bring into the dealership.
Top salespeople maximize each up they take. They are efficient and ruthlessly effective with each up they field.

To do this, they answer the basic questions each customer has left when they show up on the lot or the phone. And they do not create hurdles by needlessly chatting the customer up. They simply address what the customer wants to know and by doing this offer solutions and are helpful.

They are not perceived as a "pushy-salesman"—though they are, in fact, the pushiest salesperson there is. Exploiting each up for all the potential it holds is and always will be a license to print money.

Lose Fewer Deals

A salesman ask me when I worked for a consulting company "so how are you going to increase our sales by advertising more or what"

I answered him by saying this "we are going to increase our sales by educating our sales crew on how to do a more thorough job of closing every up we are getting now, increase sales by educating everybody on how to stop losing deals that we are losing now, we will be educating everybody on how to deliver a higher % of the approved deals that we don't get delivered now, how to stop back outs".

We also plan on educating all salespeople on where they can get sales we are currently not going after that are just sitting and waiting for us to come get. I want to see us handle this increase first. We can get an immediate increase in sales now by taking complete care of the customers we have closed and written up until they are delivered, we got now completely

We already have a lot of sales; we need to stay focused on every sale until that sale is delivered completely. A sale is a write-up until it is completely delivered. Many times, a salesman will relax after a deal is written up thinking the sale is done.

This is not the time to relax, this is the time to stay focused, watching over everything taking place on the deal. I have seen many deals lost because of something that is said to customer, a misunderstanding, a bad decision gets made about spot delivery. I have seen customers sent home in the trade-in to get the trade title and never return. Stay focused until your sale is delivered and done.

CHAPTER 2

Becoming a "Shopper Stopper"

Do not burn through ups. When a customer walks on the lot or picks up the phone to call a salesperson, they are looking for something. Until they find it, they will continue to look, to shop. Each call or customer you wait on is a potential sale, and there are only so many sales walking around, from lot to lot, looking for a salesperson to give them want they are looking for. As I like to think of it, each up is looking for a shopper-stopper.

I approach every customer from the mindset of making them a long-term client. When you talk to a customer, you should approach it from the understanding that this sale is the first of many; you are building a future with this customer. I will go more into that with my next book **Take No Ups Sell More Cars**. When you think about it from that perspective, you will find yourself providing helpful, useful answers. Instead of gimmicks or other opportunistic sales games, you will find yourself truly ensuring this car or truck fits the customer's needs—including their financial needs. Becoming a shopper-stopper requires you following these rules:

Rule 1: Understand your customer's needs

Rule 2: Know what you are selling.

Rule 3: Have a good attitude.

Rule 4: Work every deal the same way

Rule 5: Use the system

Each of these rules is addressed in subsequent chapters, so I will not belabor the points here. It suffices to say, over the years I have consistently proven that these rules, when followed, yield results.

Jim: Believed in the System

I met Jim at a place I frequented, he was a bartender. He asked me about coming to work for me selling cars. I told him I would give it some thought. I wanted to watch him interact with customers. He was an easy guy to like with a demeanor that indicated a genuine interest in what people were talking about, a good listener with an easy-going pleasant demeanor. He reminded me of a TV host named Wink Martindale, so I nicknamed him Wink. He is still called that today some 30 plus years later.

The way a salesperson talks to people is especially important today, especially regarding women. Wink was a total flirt and that scared me. He was a natural I thou but if he used that body language at the dealership it would be a big problem that I was not willing to deal with. So, I told him. I was overly impressed by how he listened to what I said and gave precise answers. He said "what is important to me is I want to be in sales, successful and I know I can be if given the chance. I would always be professional in every way" I believed him.

The first day he started he caught an up, a mother and daughter looking for daughter a car. He was eager and enthusiastic. These two traits will carry any salesperson a long way. I was keeping a close eye on him while realizing he was easy to coach. He did a great job on the deal and we ended up delivering the car for a good profit.

I told him afterword if he could conduct himself under the same attitude with that level of enthusiasm, he would do great. He said he wanted me to teach him the best way to work a deal that gets him results like today. He said, "my goal will be to always work every customer exactly like you say boss" and that is exactly what he did every time on every deal. He became a role model for others.

He believed in the system and he lived and operated within the system resulting in a high income. He seemed scared to deviated away from the system. Scared if he deviated away from the system, he would not get the great results month in and month out like he was getting now. He loved making sales and did not want them to drop off. He believed working within the system made that happen, and he was correct. His attitude of working every deal under the same set of principles got the results he wanted. He was right again.

Jim became particularly good at slowing his customers down by just visiting with them. He often said this part of the system was his favorite because it made him comfortable with the customer and the customer comfortable with him. He was consistently one of the highest-earning salesmen at the dealership.

He came with me about a year later to another dealership as a sales manager and did a great.

David: Worked the System Correctly

David was one of the most serious young men I have ever hired. He had never sold cars before. He was quiet and looked me in the eyes the entire time I was teaching them. It was not an uncomfortable look but more like a poker face that had me wondering what he was thinking. He rarely asks questions. He did smile a lot which seemed to make me wonder even more what he was thinking.

When I let him on the floor to start taking ups I found out he was serious for sure. He followed all instructions just like I told him. He asks questions and listened closely to the response from me and the customer. I never had a salesperson that intense but was beginning to like it a lot.

He always handled every up just like he was showed and was as good at slowing a customer down as anyone I worked with. He would sit down customer and family visit a while then come tell me all about what they were looking for as well as all the information needed to work the deal to the max.

He sold close to 20 cars month in and month out. He eventually became a finance manager which did not surprise me. I was sure happy to have him. He is an example of what happens when a salesperson is disciplined in following the system.

Calvin: Fought the System

Calvin was a young man that was always looking for a reason to say this customer is different. He said he did not want to be their friend just sell them a car.

He never seemed to grasp that it made the sale a lot easier to make if you let them buy.

He wanted to know all the tricks to close a customer He had been with us 3 weeks without getting a sale. He would burn an up then come tell me they had to leave because of this reason or that. I was trying to get him to simply slow the customers down by visiting.

He would find every reason in the world why a customer had to leave. This was one of those you could not be Slowed Down. I was sure if he would just start sitting down and visit with customers, he could see positive results.

I had seen many salespeople over the years get a sale they did not think they would get because they slowed the customer down enough to let them buy. That would turn the light bulb on, then it would be off to the races.

I was approaching the point Calvin needed to put on some big boy pants or I would cut him loose. I knew if he would quit thinking he had to come up with the answers and accept the answers that were already right in front of him he would start making sales.

I had seen many salespeople over the years that learning to slow a customer down did not come easy. The ones that kept working at it until they got it became better closers. I believed Calvin could be another one of those. All that having been said it was up to him to reach down inside himself and face down issues that were holding him back. Everybody is entitled to a mistake, but he was starting to abuse the privilege.

He came to me wanting to buy a Firebird we traded for. It was a special car that a lady bought new from us 3 years ago.

It had only a few thousand miles on it and was perfect in every way. I told him he could buy it but it wasn't going to be cheap as it is a very rare high-grade car. I said because of this it will sell for way above the average price of one the same year make and model.

It is important to learn that this is the kind of facts that should always be pointed out during a walk around the presentation. I went on to tell him the history of the car itself as well as all service records are right here in our shop. He said he understood. anybody wanting this car does so because it is so far above all the rest.

He wanted to go to his local bank to get a loan.so I told him most little banks like that have a habit of wanting to go by average book value and this car was going to sell way over average book value, so you need to be prepared to deal with that situation. He said no doubt he could handle all that no problem. I told him I would let him do his paperwork and let him get credit for the sale, his first. He loved that. I figured it could be a win for him all way around.

He left to go to the bank with all the paperwork. I got a call from Calvin about an hour later saying the banker said the car was overpriced and wanted to know much I was willing to lower the price. He said the banker stated the car was way over book value and I needed to give him an employee discount.

It was clear to me Calvin handled this the same way he handled push back from customers. He let the banker be the used car expert and had lost control of his deal. He had not explained the things that justified this car selling for over average book value. I considered the things the banker said to show no respect to Calvin and Calvin was letting him do it.

Calvin did not have any push back in him to explain why the price was high. No courage to put forth the demand for his due respect.

I was thinking about how many customers he reacted to in this same way. How many times did he not use the things I told him to use? The help I gave him never made it to the customer in the booth. How many times did he take the customers' position to not buy now instead of doing and saying things he should have? I realized I had allowed this young man to waste my time and energy.

I said to Calvin I am going to let you choose which one of two options you take at this point. Option 1 is put on some big boy pants and go back into that banker's office and tell him to give you a bank check for the selling price on the buyer order.

And from now forward you will do as your told when it comes to customers, exactly as told.

The second option is to come back to the dealership with a box to put all your office stuff in because you will not be working here any longer unless you can complete option one. I then hung the phone up.

He came back with a check

I thought maybe now

He will start to understand
CHAPTER 3

Understand Your Customer

You must know your customer. Knowing your Customer and your product (see Rule 2) allows you to add value by matching your customer to the right car. It may sound a lot more difficult than it really is. This is a situation of slowing your customer down enough that they will be open to you. If you get them to talk long enough every customer will tell what they will buy and what options, they are open to.

There are want buyers, need buyers, get me done buyers, monthly payment buyers and down payment buyers and many more types. My goal is to always find out what kind of buyer they are. If I know this, I have important information on what they will buy today as well as how do I put the deal together. It really is not rocket science; it is only common sense. You are not trying to get the customer to pick a wife to just pick a car they will drive for a while.

By the way it varies from year to year but most customer keep a new car an average of 27 months. The better you get at slowing the customer down the higher your closing ratio will be. If you are selling cars in a Special Finance dealership you always want to sit down with customer to find out what you are working with first. This helps the salesman put the customer on the unit that works best to put the deal together.

It is the same principle for a cash buyer. If you can sit down with the customers and just visit you will be able to find out the what the answers are you need. This is how you become a high percentage closer. You will get the customer to feel comfortable and warm up to you. Always be aware though the interview process is the same the questions are different with a cash buyer, good credit buyer and a Special Finance buyer. What makes the closing ratio go up from the visit/interview you learn what kind of customer you have. It is also especially important that you realize you cannot talk to a person that can buy anything the same way as a get me done.

This is the reason why as sales manager I separated the budget cat salesperson, the Special Finance salesman, the high line salesperson and the used car salesman.

This avoided problems during the interview of upsetting a customer. Many salespeople wrongly believe the use of the same sales system mean different the types of customer/buyers are treated to the same process.

The interview

will tell what type buyer/customer you have, so you will know how to proceed. That is why the interview/visit designed to slow the customer down is so important. The better you are at getting to know your customer the higher percent of them you will close on first try.

When you can get to know your customer's wants, needs and ability to buy, then you are in control.

Get as Much Information as possible

It is the salespersons job to make sure the sales manager and finance department get the best, most accurate information so they can properly work your deal. This includes credit applications absolutely complete no blanks and payoff information verified correct including all ads on finance contract that can be canceled. Get Copy of finance contract of trade-in

I have put countless deals together and delivered a unit other said could not buy or could not be delivered by canceling items on the finance contract. This lowers the payoff or gives customer a refund to use for down payment. That is why I like to see the customers trade-in finance contract. Always verify the payoff received includes these items have been canceled. It happens all the time that the dealer pays off a trade-in finance contract with items not cancelled. Another way to make a deal or keep from losing a deal.

Salespeople burning through ups

Looking for the one he

Wants is the same as it has always been

Bad for everybody

The sale most often blown is "The Lay Down"

One salesperson taking to many ups

Hurts the dealer by losing customers

Takes money from the other salespeople

Help Your Deal Deliver

Never Give up to Quickly

Be willing to spend however

Much time it takes

Spend all day if needed

Do that every day

You will close a lot more deals

Sell a lot more cars

Make a lot more Money

Chapter 4

Know what you are Selling

Another way salespeople provide value is by being an expert on the products you sell. There is simply no trick or way around the hard work of becoming an expert on the cars you are selling.

If you are selling new cars, you probably have a lot more resources available. If you sell used cars, you may have to do some homework. Fortunately, in the information age, information about every car sold across the United States is widely available on your computer, tablet, and phone. You just need to put in the work. I do not have to be an expert on every car or truck, but I have always kept up a general what is good about this model or that make.

A **New Car Salesman** should be able to deliver a Professional High Energy Walk Around Presentation on every new model sold by your dealerships. If you want to be the best and highest-paid salesperson then you must do what the best highest paid pros do, make people want your product. All salesmen should be entering walk around contest local, regional, and national. Like I said you want to be the best then compete with the best. Every salesperson should get themselves certified by the manufacturer and have the certification on their business cards.

All these things serve to present you in the highest possible light to customers.

Dealership Presentation

You need to deliver a presentation of two to three minutes that includes awards the dealership has earned. How important customer satisfaction and customer repeat business is.

Used Car Walk Around Presentation

are important also. You may have to research specialty models, but you can find the information on the internet. There is general information on a used car such as Front Wheel Drive and similar stuff you can use. It's also a big plus to be familiar with the history of a used car such as previous customer trade-in and stuff like that. Customers eat this up. Make sure you know the facts when talking about a car's history.

Confident people like doing business with Confident people

Educated people like doing business with Educated people.

Rise above and stay away from the actions and mentality typical of so many car salespeople.

A strong enthusiastic **Walkaround Presentation** will raise your closing average....

Every day you should warm up doing your walk around

Practice your walk around presentation just like you were delivering it to a customer. Always listen to yourself when practicing your walk around, even better, record it and play it back listening for ways to say the same thing with even more enthusiasm and conviction. It is better if you sound like you believe it

Practice Makes Perfect

How you say things are just as important as

What you say

Kill Them with Kindness

You start closing a deal the moment you make contact. Always have a bounce in your step, be sincere when greeting customers. Always Smile Enthusiasm and Smiling are two important things you must always include. Manufacturers Walk Arounds build excitement and teach you how to encourage buyers to buy now.

You should learn to do a great walk around the presentation even if your dealership does not encourage it. After all, it is your **Paycheck**

Chapter 5

Have a good attitude

"The only limits a person has are the ones they put on themselves"

Johnny Mack Jones

Attitude is critical. A Good Attitude will make people like you before they get to know you. A good attitude is required to be successful at anything. Attitude changes everything. A good attitude is a required foundation to build your success upon. A great attitude alone makes the sky the limit. Tricks, Smoke and Mirrors, or gimmicks will get you sales Some of the time.

But that is a technique used by few successful car dealers—and all carnival workers. I have worked with many salesmen and many sales managers using these techniques and the results were always the same. "Take Less Ups - Sell More Cars" approach will result in a lot more sales; a lot more money; and a lot more repeat and referral sales with a much higher CSI score.

A good attitude will make you consistently lucky. There is a fine line between success and failure. Attitude is that invisible fine line. People want a pleasant buying experience. They are spending thousands of dollars for a car, a very personable possession. The more interesting and informative facts you can share with them the more they enjoy the buying experience.

Most buyers easily recognize when a salesperson believes what he is saying and respond favorably. It is the invisible fine line that determines whether you make the sale or not every time.

Customers recognize the negatives of a Salesperson

Flirtatious behavior toward women; impatience with indecisiveness; condescending attitude; hard confrontational payment/finance qualifying; or not listening to a customer are but a few of the behavior's customers say made them leave a dealership.

Never Miss A Chance Wrecker Driver

I left a joint in the ashtray of my demo, causing my removal as Used Car Manager; demoted to salesman; and working under a fellow determined to make it as hard as possible on me so I would quit. He did not like the fact the owner asks me to stay and sell cars nor was he aware the owner had promised my job back when things cooled off.

On my first day back on the floor, I was the last salesman to leave for the day. I had sold a car and since I had to give up my new demo, I needed something to drive. I went to the manager to borrow a used car to drive home. He handed me the keys to an old Trans Am trade-in telling me, "I've got a special driver for you". It was raining hard. When I found the car, the old piece of junk door handles was broke, making it difficult to get in; the T Tops were busted and leaking; the seats were wet; the dash lights were out; and the battery was dead.

I lived an hour away and driving home I could hardly see because the defroster did not work, and the wipers were bad. Making matters more frustrating halfway home the car stopped running way out in the country.

I coasted into an old closed store and called a wrecker. Since it was his last tow for the night the wrecker driver asked if he could take me home; leave the car hooked up; come get me at 8 am on his way to the dealership.

The next morning, he showed up with a buddy of his and they began asking me about buying a car. We got to the dealership, dropped the car in service, and then went to look at cars. By 9:30 the driver and his friend had both selected a car and by 10:30 I had two car deals done. I made a point to thank the new manager for creating the opportunity. He said, "you are the luckiest SOB I've ever known."

Take Less Ups Sell More Cars

It is a way of thinking system to discipline you to Slow Customers Down. Employing basic selling skills like introducing yourself to everybody present including spouse, friend, or children, and calling them by name are powerful ways to slow a customer down. My system works in any city in any state at any Dealership. I'm so sure of it I'm willing to bet my $5000 against your $50 that if you honestly and tenaciously learn and apply my Take Less Ups Sell More Cars you will sell more cars and make more money.
Isn't it better operating in a manner that makes the buying experience more enjoyable for your customer? Also gets your CSI surveys to consistently receive the highest scores possible

Proof Is in the Pudding

I recently visited 25 car dealers to see how the sales team treated each person who entered the door. I would like to have seen the salespeople introduce themselves to each person who walked in the door, not just the person who appeared to be the head of their party.

However, I was not surprised to find that most of the salespeople were only shaking hands and introducing themselves with the person perceived to be the decision-maker of the party. Sadly, I only found 3 salespeople who introduced themselves to the entire party.

Trying to hurry up through the introduction process to get a sale will rarely get you a sale but will lose sales instead Customers will warm up to you and become comfortable if you use simple introduction skills.

The Concept or Taking Less Ups Sell More Cars is done by employing simple sales skills most every salesperson already knows. Starting with a proper introduction then methodically slowing the customer down until you go thru the only 3 options for an up: 1) find a unit in your inventory he likes well enough to buy; 2) show him alternative units that he likes well enough to buy; or 3) locate a unit he likes well enough to buy. There are no other alternatives. This process requires time with the customer. The more time spent with the customer the higher the closing ratio.

A salesperson who quick-qualifies customers has a high percentage of easy sales blown while looking for an "easy" sale. Slowing every customer down enough to walk thru all options result in a much higher closing percentage.

The concept explains there are easier and better places to sell a car than waiting for an up at the dealership. That is the basic concept of how you Take Less Ups Sell More Cars. Also, how to avoid losing a deal due to miscues by yourself as well as others. By working a deal through you will close more, deliver more, and make more money.

Sell two Cars at the Same Time

I have known salesmen that have sold for years and never did a deal selling two units on the same deal. Then again, I have known salespeople who have had two deals at once, month-in and month-out. Is it Just Luck? No way!
If you believe it as the normal that's what it will become. Remember, I am not talking about a customer referring a sale to you but two deliveries during the same visit

Slowing a customer down and getting to know everybody in the party will let you know if there are two deals here. I have done it lots of times and found when I do my job with the 1st one right the 2nd one is an easy sale. You ask for the 2nd sale just like you normally do the 1st.
Anytime a co-signer is involved or needed is a perfect opportunity. This is especially true when co-signer is needed but uses the objection "I plan to buy me a car soon, but cosigning will keep me from being able to." That is a perfect occasion to suggest we do both deals right now followed up with a couple of sales points such as I can even get buyer #1 a referral fee/gift and throw in a special something for you. Plus, it simplifies the financing for both of you.

What a great story you both will have for years to come about the day you two bought two cars at the same time, same dealership, awesome. Some of that is the kind of stuff I would say you have to choose your words your way. The simple discipline of watching for the opportunity

Chapter 6

Outside Sales

Sell Cars Outside Dealership

Selling cars outside the dealership is the most overlooked way to get sales. It is also the easiest close you will ever encounter. The more you adjust to outside sales the higher percentage you will close. As I worked to learn how to do an effective and tenacious follow-up, I discovered outside sales is a great way to follow-up and close at the same time. We had a truly little walk-in traffic at the dealership I started at so the things I learned fast: prospect, close, follow-up; outside sales; and follow-up.

Once you sell a car away from dealership at home business or farm you will never be the same, I promise you. Customers are more comfortable in their environment.

Why Doesn't Every Dealership Do Outside Sales?

Great question since the moral of these stories is obvious. Yet, I worked for an auto consulting company in numerous dealerships all over America and rarely found outside sales being made. Only a few commercial/fleet departments I found few practiced outside sales. Matter of fact most never heard of selling cars like that

. I encountered salespeople that did not understand how you could sell a vehicle on the outside, even got asked if that was legal. All the outside sales I told you about above are regular retail deals that maintain a high gross profit well above dealership average.

It Works on Every Level

I used the same format as a wholesale car dealer and sold 20 cars the 1st day I started calling on New Car Dealers in Nashville, TN. I would take a car and go from dealership to dealership sometimes selling the car I was driving sometimes I sold other cars I had available. It is still the same approach.

Trade-in Row

A Great Place to Start Every Day

My 1st stop when I got to the dealership every morning was trade-in row. I was looking for something I had a customer looking for or something I could go finds somebody to buy and that is a long list. Unusual and unique vehicles were the easiest units to find a buyer for. Many guys I worked with called them queer cars that would be hard to sell at the dealer auction much less retail buyer.

I looked at those units as easy because they were outside the normal or hard to find trade-ins such as heavy-duty pickups like many small construction companies would use or an individual who pulled a race car with or a pickup with service bed. The easiest of them all was and still is a cheap car or pickup. I would get in one of these, drive around asking people if they knew anybody that needed a cheap vehicle.

Easy Sale this way heavy-duty pickups were easy Sales at construction sites vans and box trucks to companies that are too small to buy new and Cadillac's and Lincolns at Funeral Homes. So many different examples I could tell you about it is a way of thinking.

It is Easier to Close Outside Sales?

Always Have Paperwork with You To Write up the deal just like you do in the dealership. There is no difference between the flow of paperwork in an outside sale and a sale made at the dealership. After you do a couple of outside sales you will see this. The advantages for F&I far outnumber any disadvantages. Most deals sold outside the store have the customer come in to "Settle Up"

A Top Cadillac Salesman in America

I had the pleasure of working with a guy who was one of the top Cadillac salesmen in America. He had been #1 a couple of years and in the top 10 for many years in a row. Every morning at the sales meeting as sales were announced he would have at least one and sometimes two or three sales. I wondered where he got all those sales especially since I rarely saw him in the dealership. He was always at a golf tournament or some event it seemed like.

I asked him one day about getting sales from folks that do not come in and purchase at the dealership. I was shocked when he said under no circumstances would he ever go back to selling at the dealership. "That's a tough way to do it, way too hard for me," he said. I much prefer closing in an office, living room, or on a golf cart

A Top Ford Truck Salesmen

West Texas is the most sparsely populated area in America, yet its home turf to one of America's top Ford salesman. You will not find him hanging around the store waiting for an up.

He comes into the dealership in the mornings for an hour or so before heading out to farms, ranches, businesses, and homes to sell Fords.

He does come in on Saturdays for appointments only. Ask if he is concerned about missing a customer at the dealership? His answer is, "No, I'm more concerned about missing a sale out in the field."

He sells a lot of pickups at feedlots in barns out in the field and just about any other place you could think of. He consistently maintains a high gross profit on his sales.

He gets full retail, not fleet prices.
He said closing deals this way is so much more personal.

Top Producing Mercedes Benz Salesmen

If I ask you where you think one of the top Mercedes Benz salesmen in America lives you would say, Los Angeles, New York, Miami, Chicago, Atlanta, or Washington DC. The fact is these would be correct if you included Columbia MO with those other cities. This story rings close to home for me because he worked for me. I met him after he had spent a year in the car business.

He told me he earned around $36,000 during that first year. I explained how to use outside sales and prospecting along with a country boy style customer service to sell and close Benz deals and he was receptive, even excited about it. The 1st sale he made outside the dealership was a new Mercedes. He closed it sitting at their dining room table. He was so excited about closing more deals like that. "The easiest sale I ever made!", he said. "This is the way I want to do it!"

He also made more commission on that sale than his average MONTHLY earning for the previous year. His income was well over six figures the next year. He built an impressive customer client base using this system customizing it to his personality.

Most people are simply more comfortable on their turf. Walking into a dealership can be very intimidating to a lot of folks. Outside sales work because it personalizes the buying experience, removes the distractions of a dealership, allows a customer to more comfortably look over a vehicle, people are less likely to negotiate a price you give them, and the customer takes mental ownership of the vehicle while sitting in their yard.

Outside Prospecting Sales Work

Outside Prospecting/Sales should be an important part of your daily work schedule. Outside prospecting using donuts/coffee etc. should be assigned a specific day and time so they know to expect you there in person. You should always share an enthusiastic greeting to all there and remind them you have a couple of slots open for appointments if they have a referral for car sale (it is a joke).

Outside the dealership personal prospecting appearances yield tremendous sales results when done properly.

I bet you could think of 10 places to prospect at and develop referrals. Beauty shops and Barbershops are great. Insurance companies and body shops constantly are dealing with people needing cars and make great places to get referrals from. These are much less difficult to close.

Be One of the Best

Outside prospecting/selling in person along with 10 daily prospecting phone calls will pay off big time in sales and commission. It is how you can become one of the elite highest paid car salesmen in America.

I aim to close an extremely high percentage of ups at the dealership on 1st visit. This means pulling out all stops and reducing actions that lose deals. Included in this way of working is staying with customers all through deals including going with them to get others involved in decision making.

Customer Follow-up in Person

A specific trade-in/unit arrives that a customer has been looking for. The best way to handle this is to get in it and drive it to them.

The Best Way to Prospect

How When and Where

I learned how important prospecting and outside sales were from working in a small town. Today it is even more important yet rarely done at dealerships. I later found that it worked well in any size city and any brand dealership. Here are some of the ways that worked for me.

Free Coffee Once A Week

I would host free coffee at a little cafe one day a week from 5 am to 7 am. I paid for coffee for farmers, ranchers, businessmen, or anybody that wanted to sit in my section. I visited with them about cars, trucks, and whatever. I made appointments, got referrals, and made sales right there in the cafe especially new Ford pickups.

Doughnut Day

I visited people I knew mainly in their business. I brought donuts to a different business each day of the week, Insurance Company on Monday, a barber on Tuesday, etc. I guarantee you they knew what day doughnut day for them and was always ready and grateful to me for those delicious fresh-baked donuts.

I did this, so they would return the favor by referring people to me that wanted or needed to buy a vehicle. I always left a business card and took a few minutes to say hi and visit. This was especially effective with insurance offices and body shops.

Be Who They Come to Buy From

Insurance offices on several occasions would have a buyer comes in to meet with me at their office on doughnut day. That group sold more cars for me than any bird dog (referral) I ever had. Company policy prevented them from accepting bird dog pay but they were quick to remind me of their favorite doughnut/pastry which I was happy to include.

They knew they were my best bird dogs, going so far as to calling their doughnut orders in for me to pick up when they sent me deals. It was fun, I made friends there. Choose your Doughnut places carefully making sure they understand you are doing this, so they will always remember to refer your sales opportunities.

Spend More Time *Selling*

The easiest sale to close is the one most often lost. This is the customer you did not do all you could have done to close. You let him go and he went down the street .

Closing

What Is A Close? It is the process of buying. You start closing when they walk in the door. You begin closing from hello. You are starting to close when you slow them down. Learn to visit with the customer.

The easiest customer to close is the sale most often lost

Be willing to spend as much time as needed

You will Sell More Cars - If you Take Less Ups

People Love Stories

Tell More Stories Close More Deals

I have got more stories than any normal salesman
A mother and daughter could not decide on what color mustang for the daughter. I said "you know last week I had a similar situation in that a parent loved the car but preferred a different color than daughter, so I said why don't you buy both colors one for you and the other for her and you know what? That is exactly what ended up happening. They bought both". They laughed, and the mother said, "So are we".

Ask All the Right Questions - Get All the Right Answers

How Not to Blow a Deal?

I was working at a Cadillac dealership and watched a salesman greet a well-dressed couple and their teenage daughter. They drove up in a nice Cadillac that was about 3 years old. Before I could finish smoking my cigarette, I saw them come out heading toward their car with a steam trail behind them. I cut them off and spoke politely asking did they not see anything they liked. Turns out they wanted a deal where they could trade in their current Cadillac on a new Cadillac and buy a new small car for their daughter. They wanted to finance both with GMAC where they financed the last 5 new Cadillacs they bought. The salesman wanted them to decide which 1 they wanted to buy today.

He told them since the wife had retired from teaching and just the husband worked, he felt like buying two cars was unlikely to get financed. He insisted they buy 1 car today so it would be a lot easier to get done. He had not even taken a credit application, their credit was as close to perfect as could be, he was not aware the husband's income was $150,000 a year, the wife had a retirement income of $2000 a month and the Cadillac being traded in was paid off. He was so insistent on doing it his way the customer got upset and so did salesman, so they got up and walked out. I apologized and said I sell used cars would you consider 1-year old low mileage program Cadillac and a 1-year old low mileage program Chevrolet that we made a special purchase of. They looked they liked it. Turns out that paid-off trade-in was appraised at $10,000, his $150.000 a year, and nearly perfect credit score made for two easy sales. While they were out on a demo ride, I went to the showroom and looked on the up log. The salesman had written "wants two new cars before they repossess the one, he is driving, what a flake" In less than 1 hour I had a 2-car deal was approved signed and delivered.

Farmer Story

A young salesman was struggling to turn over every customer. He always wanted to explain to me why the c/s left - Ma & Paw drove into lot riding up and down lines. Salesman took the up but could not get them to get out of their pickup. I noticed they spent a lot of time staring at a Town n Country Wagon. They told him this was the 1st dealer they stopped at and they were going to look around other car lots to see what was available and would come back to see the ones they liked.

They were driving around to leave I saw Jeff running toward the showroom, so I stepped outside and stopped them.

The farmer stopped to talk to me with the truck in drive and his foot on the brake. He and his wife admitted they liked the T-C Wagon and might come back to look closer. I finally got him to put the truck in the park- then to turn the ignition off. The farmer and his wife still would not get out, I sent the salesman to go get Wagon and pull it up next to farmer's pickup.

I began an enthusiastic walk around asking for comment and agreement from both. They were still in the truck, so I ask him "would you work for me here at an easy job for $100 an hour" he said yea, so I hired him to test drive that Wagon 15 minutes for 25 cash. After a couple of minutes laughing at the idea, I pulled out $25 and they got out of the truck to take the Wagon for a test drive. When they came back, they came inside and wrote a check for it.

1st Day 1st Up 1st Sale

I figured I would watch the other salesman see what they do until I figured it out. One of the biggest snowstorms ever had hit the night before my 1st day selling cars. With the snow about 3 feet deep, I sat in the used car office with the 4 older salesmen who kept asking me questions with suspicion. They kept telling me how bad things were in the car business. One of them said, "Well here you go. We're going to let you have the first customer of the day", they laughed. I tried to defer the customer back to them, but they would have no part of it.

I walked outside to see a fellow in his early 20's that had walked onto the lot. He had long wiry hair and I thought he looked like a biker guy maybe. As I got close, I noticed he was wearing sandals with a light windbreaker and had his arm in a cast.

I introduced myself trying my best to sound like a real car salesman. He said, "Well at least here somebody is going to come out and wait on me. I just left the car lot down the street and they just stared at me through the window, never came out, so I left." I did not know the procedure, so I ask what he was trying to buy.

He began to tell me his story of leaving his wife and a small baby in western KS after the packing plant he worked at shut down. He left the only car they owned with his wife, caught a bus here; rented a room; and got a job at Winchester Packing plant.

He went on to tell me how the (other employees and his supervisor) called him hippie; would tell him to stand in a certain spot only to have a frozen half a cow come flying in and knock him down which they thought was funny.
He was not used to this automation because they did not have it at his old plants. He said he walked to work in the snow and freezing weather. Coworkers would pass him but not stop and offer a ride.

Then one guy said for him to hold this which he did, and a saw flew by before he could get his arm out of the way it nearly cut his arm off. He then said I just came from the lawyer's office Johnny I have $12,000 in cash, and I want to buy this VW right here if you will let me.

I did not know what to do next, so I took him in to the office to find the price of the car, collect his money and go from there. I had not seen the money but did not doubt the guy. We entered the used car office where I ask what the price of the VW was. One salesman said $6995 and laughed (the real price was $3995) I said great you got that much right, he said yea, how much with tax and everything though I still had not seen money - so I ask how much with the tax and all, they said 3%.

We added up the total price including the tax on a piece of paper and he began counting out money.

I could tell there was something wrong in that office, they were not happy for me. He ask "when do I get the title" of course, I did not have a clue. Customer said fill out the paperwork, so I can drive it home to my wife she loves those cars. I asked salesman say how do yawl do your paperwork here - one responded I thought you sold cars before - I said yea - but someone else did the paperwork - a different one of them said here let's help the new guy. He said take him to Burt's office upstairs (Burt is the owner) he is the one that does the all paperwork for you.

I scooped up the money and my new hippie friend and went upstairs. We found the owner walking out of his office as we came up. I told him this guy is buying the VW. I need you to do all the paperwork for me because he is ready to take it back to western Kansas and give it to his wife today, here is the cash with tax and all.

The owner stood silent looking stunned at me and the customer then asks" why did you bring him to me" I said the other salesman told me you do all the paperwork - a moment of silence again before the owner said well come on in and let's get it done.

My customer noticed the expensive cigars on his desk and asks for one since he just bought a car. I ask him for one since I just sold my first car. The owner gave us both one and lit it up for us. The three of us sat there smoking Cuban cigars laughing like it was a party I thought this selling car stuff is a great job. I noticed the other salesman kept walking by his door looking surprised by all the fun we were having.

The owner showed me paperwork, so I would know how to handle it in the future in case he was not there. He told me after the customer left to go to used car building and shake their hands thanking them for helping you so much. I did but they did not want to shake my hand.

Practice What You Preach

Legend - sell cars for two weeks - I was hired as a used car manager for a Mercedes Benz store by a Gen Manager I had worked for previously. I went to the dealership on the 16th of the month, met with the owner, and was hired. The owner said the used car manager I was replacing had been there for 7 years, so he wanted him to finish the month out and he would make the change on 1st. I ask what I was supposed to do for two weeks to which owner said "we will take of your room and food at the hotel next door to dealership" so you can rest up.

I told them I wanted to go on the floor for these two weeks and sell cars. The owner said, "no way what if you don't sell much then I look bad hiring you as used car manager". I said if you are worried, that I cannot hold my own as a salesperson why would you want me to be your sales manager. He agreed to this but with the condition, if I did poorly, he was free to ask himself why he would want me as his used car manager and look for someone else.
In the two weeks, I sold 12 cars, made several thousand, got to know the salesman, and made the owner look like a hero.

At the sales meeting, he announced I was hired to be the used car manager. He said it was his idea to have me work on the floor to prove myself to the sales crew.

I Got the Last Laugh

I was in a habit of always being 10-15 minutes late every day. My manager & friend Danny decided to have some fun with it so he said we had to come in at 7 am to help move all used cars off the lot so the sweeper machine could clean it then put the cars back. He emphasizes be here at 7 am sharp so we could be sure to get it done.

I arrived about 6:45 that morning and decided to go ahead and start moving them since no one else was there. Around 7:15 I was still the only one there and was wondering where everybody else was.

A pickup pulled into the lot. The fellow said he would love to buy this Dodge pickup on our display rack but he worked from before we opened until after we closed and ask if we could we make a deal. He asked why I was there so early so I told him why, and he said Thank God for that, so I can buy this truck I been wanting.

About 8:50 Danny pulled up and ask what the hell was I doing, explaining I went ahead and moved all the cars for the sweeper machine to be able to work the lot. He said that it was just a joke they were playing on me since I was always late. He said we figured you would not show up. I thanked him for the opportunity his joke created when I showed him my sale of the Dodge truck. We had a great laugh.

Dealer Did Not Like Me

I guess I can be an easy guy to dislike. Moral of this story OK there is no moral I just like it and it is also true. The consulting company I worked for sent me to a dealership that the general manager was in dealer development.

He had a speech impediment and a habit of pointing at his open hand with a finger when explaining something as though what he was talking about was written on his palm. He hated me some of that was because GMAC made him hire us to train the salespeople when he felt like he could do it.

But he was making it personal because our company had sent me. I was miserable so I called my boss to ask if he would replace me and send somebody else to this dealership. He said no I needed to figure out how to solve and overcome the issues with him and make things work, calling it a good healthy challenge that would make me better at my job.

It was the 1st nonsmoking dealership I had ever been to. I was on the smoking site of the showroom standing under a small awning when a pickup truck pulled up in the beating down raining. The driver rolled his window down and asks me where the parts department was. I pointed, and he pulled away.

I heard a pounding on the glass and turned to see GM going berserk motioning for me to come there. I did, and he began to rip my head off about the pickup he saw me talk with briefly. He was screaming in front of the entire sales crew about how I, a so-called expert was observed brooming an up by his entire sales force.

He began pointing to his palm again with his finger saying it cost him $120 for every customer that pulled up to the dealership and I had just cost him $120. I said that's not true he was asking for parts, he said you don't make exceptions for these guys and you just set a bad example plus you cost me a $120. I said no I did not, yes you did he screamed

. I said no I did not, there were two people in that truck it cost you $240. Well, he helped me get my transfer I wanted the same day.

Never Give Up on a Deal

Get Your Credit Turndowns Delivered

Somebody Will Finance Them

Relative's friend's small-town banks are always good possibilities to get **Financing** **Outside Source Financing** such as credit unions, small loan companies also are good **Outside Source Financing**

1. Just because regular or **Special finance** departments could not get your deal approved does not mean your deal is dead.
2. It simply means it is time for you to find **Outside Source Financing** and I guarantee you a high percent of your T D can get done this way.

You need to find any place they or their family has done credit business. Find if a relative can buy for them at their bank – not a straw purchases this way we are not involved and many times a relative will step in and help them.

Most small-town banks do not care. They do not use a credit score to determine a loan approval. They will do loans based their knowledge of customer or a personal relationship with customer or customers family. Some do not report credit bureau, and some will not give a reference. But many of them will loan your customer the money when no one else will

Take Proper Credit Application

That would be an application with no blank spaces written in print or type in clear legible form. Be sure it also is COMPLETE in that all income is accurately and honestly stated, and information is precise. It is also good to include a blank sheet of paper with any additional financial information concerning customers. I never understood why anybody would turn a poorly filled out credit application in. I see salespeople and managers alike just refuse to get in line on this simple task, even heard you got the social address and work they do not need all that stuff.

I work with a desk manager who was great at working deal except he turned partially filled out apps in on almost every deal none were ever complete. So, I would send them into GMAC like that, the ones they approved where they would get a low tier by GMACs MAPS System and a lower than needed amount approved due to missing information.

I would notify him of call or qualification which was often lower than requested so he had to restructure deal (cut it), which he would do and give it back to me still despite my asking him to complete the application.

I would get customers in F&I office get all the missing information on the application, resend it to GMAC asking for new tier consideration, most time getting it then soak up all the profit he gave up into my department.

I never understood how a guy so smart could act so stupid That's why it is so important for you get all info can on credit application. It always helps your deal to have completed credit apps. You can never have too much information

Watch for captive finance opportunities

Here is a suggestion for you when you catch a phone up inquiring about an ad that mentions payments or financing in any way:

Customer- Hey you got any of those cars for $199 a month there or is there a catch to that deal?

Salesman- (pull out an application) your complete name is and spell it for me if you would- ok day of birth- social security number and I continue filling out application completely -
Customer- why you are asking me for that

Salesman- you wanted to see if you qualify for that payment in ad correct

Customer- a high percentage of time will say ok
Salesman- continue completing application then
ask what amount they have for down payment – collect as much information as possible visit with the customer about a car, etc. and make an appointment

Customer- are you going to call me back to let me know if I qualify

Salesman- do you have good credit?
Customer= no matter what he says

Salesman – well looks good to me on this side the finance manager will want to verify your ID and info when you get here and answer all your questions – set an appointment you then get with the manager and make a deal, so you can put this deal in finance for pre-approval.

Be hard to get skated since the deal is in finance also does not matter if he forgets your name

Build Repeat Customers

You Can Sell Cars without Walk-in Ups

Take No Ups Sell Even More Cars

By building a client base then using the same tenacious approach to maintain good contact with your base you could sell enough cars through referral and repeat business that you would not even have to take any new ups except by appointment.

You should use US mail, e-mail, and all social media such as Facebook Twitter. Do a monthly Newsletter, birthday cards for the entire family – all correspondence no matter how it is delivered should end with

Tell Your Family & Friends to Always Ask for You

Be a Strong Product Salesperson

Develop an Award-Winning

Walk Around Presentation

.

Internet Sales

  Internet Customer service is no different on how you treat a customer and what questions you ask if they were in your showroom. It is just as easy to come across as good or bad as it is in person or on the phone. Recent testing of 7 Nashville dealerships websites found many of the same turns offs customers complained about in the past with salesman.

  Internet people came online during browse to ask if they could help – great technology tool BUT when asking about a rebate on a certain model all 7 ignored the question and ask for customer information. When the question was repeated 2nd time all 7 once again ignored the question and ask for customer information such as name e-mail and when they planned to buy. When asking 3rd time if they could just answer if a certain model had a rebate 5 replied they would get with internet manager to find out then ask for customer information such as e-mail phone to get back to the customer and two ended the conversation.

  None of them showed any interest in trying to just answer the question then move forward. They were all cold and calculating. Many of today's research-orientated customers consider this pushy or rude. Customers doing research want answers to questions and information., I found that when I employed the same slow methods while providing the information requested it worked great. I understood what the online salespeople were trying to do, and I wanted to get to the same place as they did. But kindness comes across online as it does in person, so does bluntness. I had a high degree of success using the same be polite while I slow the customer down the system.

Be a Team Player

The best Employees

Help your dealership

Be a great fun place to work

Get Out of Customers Way

So, They Can Buy

Laugh if you will, but this is a common mistake salesperson make. Let a customer that knows what they will buy right now do just that. I once heard a salesman say "you need to be quiet and let me explain what works for you I been selling cars a long time"

Close A Deal on the Phone

Many times, I heard grab that Johnny Mack you like to chatter on the phone followed by a laugh then a "tell them to write a check over the phone" followed by another laugh. A customer would walk in later that day asking for me then get delivered 30 minutes later. I would get asked "when did you work them" I would say oh been working with them. Reality is I took credit application for pre-approval on the phone call they were laughing about earlier but I did not want to spoil their fun

Raise the Dead Deal - Breathe Life into It

Every day you just need to deliver 1 deal. I would start every day looking for the most likely prospect that could deliver that day while waiting for an up Prospect any and every way I can I can't make a Sale visiting with my running buddy or the other salesmen so every second I think "where can I sell a car"

Small Minds Talk about People

Average Minds Talk about Events

Great Minds Talk about Ideas

When all is said and done

Attitude – Discipline - Kindness

Education - Product Knowledge

Good Time Management

Will Deliver Deals Every Day

But Old Habits are hard to Break

Here is a new Habit to start

Take Less Ups Make More Sales

Things you fail to do Will make the next

Salesperson's job a lot easier

(He Read my Book)

OVERCOME CAR SALESMANS BAD RAP

The public's perception is that most car salesman are like crooked carnival workers at a fair. You will stand out from that crowd if you apply the principles in this book.

Is This Vehicle Chicken Salad or Chicken Poop

Always Tell the Truth, The Whole Truth

And Nothing but The Truth

I have sold lots of vehicles that needed repairs as well as vehicles that needed nothing. I have sold vehicles that were junk as well as nearly perfect ones. It is OK to sell "Chicken Poop" as long as you "Clearly Represent it as such.

As a Used Car Manager, I would separate the salesmen that Sold our best, most expensive units from the salesmen that sold our budget vehicles. I did this for several good reasons.

Customers, most of the time, are two different types of buyers.

A standup high-quality vehicle with, verifiable service records, low mileage and good ownership will always bring way above average book value. It is the ones that gets a strong walk-around presentation to every customer it is shown to pointing out every one of these qualities.

If a salesman shows a lot of A grade units then shows a real nice-looking high mileage budget car that is missing a couple good qualities creates a potential bad situation. It can ruin a good reputation a salesman has earned.

Full Disclosure is Very Important

A vehicle that has been badly wrecked and repaired should be disclosed to a customer. The worse thing any salesperson can do is to describe the damage as having been a little parking lot fender bender when the damage was greater.
When you represent a vehicle as previously damaged from the start you are being a straight shooter. Dealers that get a "Builder" in on trade and clearly discloses that fact is doing things the right way.
Dealers that buy wrecked cars to fix up and sell without disclosing it is a builder are known as "Outlaw Dealers" and should be avoided by customer and the salesmen.

If You Are Willing to Make Changes
Make Them Improvements

That is My Story

I hope you genuinely enjoyed reading

Take Less Ups Sell More Cars

as much as I enjoyed writing it. If you are willing to use this book as a tool and a way of thinking pattern you will greatly increase your ability to close sales.

Remember, Sales are all about

Attitude   Discipline   Determination
If You Want It - Go Get It

The Automobile Market is and always will be Strong
You Are in Control of Your Own Destiny

Make your mind up-Refuse to be Denied
Your Will Own Your Goals

I want to Remind you how Important it is to
Always Be Aware of the Buying Power of Women customers.

Women make up a large portion of the Automobile Buying Market. They must be treated with Professional Respect and Courtesy

Love Every Customer

The Way God
Loves You

Good Luck & God Bless

My Favorite True Car Story

     I was paged to the used car showroom, as I approached the man waiting to see me, I noticed the way he was dressed. He looked like he had bought a suit at a Goodwill Store. His pants were way too short exposing a pair of worn-out old dress shoes, his shirt was wrinkled, he was wearing an old wide tie from back in the '60s. His face cheeks showed broken blood vessels like alcohol abuse will cause but he was wearing a warm smile.

     He extended his right hand to me and gave me a firm handshake as I walked up. He wanted a job as a used car salesman. I told him I would not be able to hire him, but I was curious why he came here to a big fancy high line store to apply. He named a used car lot owner that told him to come to see me because I might hire him because of his background. I told him that fellow was trying to be funny and he knew better.

     The old fellow was very polite and ask me to consider giving him a chance. He said an opportunity is all he was asking for and I will not be disappointed. He said I have a lot of experience. He said I have a story I can share with you to explain what happened to me. I said you seem like an exceptionally fine fellow, with a great smile, but I got to be straight forward and honest with you. We have a strict dress for success policy which it does not appear you could meet at this point. I thanked him for coming in and suggested he get a job at a used car lot and maybe later down the road we could talk. He kept asking for a chance in an exceedingly kind non-pushy way. He asks if I would give him 3 days to show me, he could be good productive help. He said I can handle high line customers and close deals.

I ask him what made him so sure he could close the kind of customers we get; we sell Mercedes, Cadillac, Volvo, and a few others. They draw an affluent clientele that could be reluctant to be waited on by somebody looking as you do currently.

He said he has been doing this for a long time. He said he owned a successful Toyota dealership for 25 years and just needed a chance. He said I know I do not look sharp now but if you give me a chance I will in no time at all and be a real good help for you. His tone of voice was not begging just very pleasant and seemed real. But I thought the "I used to own a successful Toyota store" for 25 years was outside of my belief.

I ask him where his Toyota store was and what happened to it. He began his story about drinking, cheating, getting divorced, and finally losing everything he had as he became a drunk.

What got me was that Toyota dealership he named was only about 80 miles from where I had spent 20 years in the car business. I remembered there were lots of stories about the owner of that dealership that pretty much matched the stories I just heard from this old man. I knew it was him. It was hard to believe that now over a decade later hundreds of miles away from there I was looking at the very man I had heard so much about back then. I knew when I shook his hand, saw that smile, and the gentle way he spoke there was something unusual about this old drunk.

However, I still did not want to put a man looking like he did on my sales team and I told him so. He kept politely grinding away about just an opportunity that is all. I offered to make some phone calls to a few used car dealers to help him get a job. Still, he kept a polite tenacity in a skillful non-combative way asking for just a 3-days opportunity.

I decided I would give him a 3-day chance to show me his mouth was not writing checks his butt could not cash. So, I gave him a list of things he better not do.
I watched as he walked out of the dealership and got in an old Cadillac that had a different color fender than the rest of the car. After he left, I wondered if I just made a mistake but there was something about him, I liked it.

The next morning at 8:30 I saw him walking up in the rain. He was wearing the very same set of clothes as I again pondered my potential mistake. I ask him where was his old Cadillac I saw him leave in yesterday. He said it was low on gas so instead of running out and being late for his first day he would walk. He said the walk lifted his spirits.

I told him to stay outside of the showroom under the large overhang, do not hang around on the showroom. I said I would take him upstairs to fill out employment papers after he sold a car and I decided to make him a permanent hire.

The sales crew comes in at 9. About 8:40 I saw a good looking 20-year-old Mercedes pull into the used car lot with an older couple in it. I watched as they pulled around to a line of used Mercedes then stopped and got out looking. I was thinking what a great up this is. The only salesman in the dealership was the old man and he headed straight to wait on them.

I felt nervous in my stomach so I stood where I could keep a close eye on them. He took one of the umbrellas that we keep by the door with him as he walked out to the customer. I watched closely as he opened the umbrella and gave it to her, then introduced himself to both while wearing a great smile. He seemed to warm up to them quickly while moving through the cars. As the other salesmen began arriving, they ask who he was and what is he doing. I said I got this.

About 30 minutes later the old salesman put momma in the back seat, pops in the front passenger seat then got in and drove up to the building asking me how to get a dealer tag for a demo ride. I gave him one and they left.

About a half-hour later they pulled back in under the covered area with momma driving, the salesman on the passenger side, and pops in the back seat. They all seem to be enjoying themselves. As they were getting out of the vehicle, I eased out of the door just in case they would start to leave. I heard the salesman say "it's easy to tell you both love this Mercedes should I get the paperwork ready" the husband replied "we want it if the price is inline, you haven't told us what the asking price is yet" salesman responded "well it's a Mercedes so it won't be cheap, but you already knew that"

The negotiations for price and trade-in went perfectly and the deal was done. I was extremely impressed with the great job the salesman did with every aspect of this deal from the meeting and greeting, demo ride, trial closes, and working the deal itself. It was textbook all the way. If there is such a thing as Perfect, I just witnessed it.

I was thinking this as the salesman left to go take the sold car to be cleaned for delivery. The customer walked up and ask if he could talk to me in private. In my office, the customer asks what was the story with the salesman? He said "I want to be perfectly clear; it was a great experience buying from this salesman, he has done a lot of sales, is very well-spoken and intelligent. An exceedingly kind respectful fellow that my wife and I really like. We just want to know his story, there has got to be one, something happened in his life"

I proceeded to tell them all I knew about him and his two years sober. The customer said they feel like he deserves some help and wanted to know if they could help him get a good wardrobe of clothes. He asks if they could write a check for $1000 but did not want to say or do anything offensive to anybody. In all the years I been in the car business I never had a customer so impressed with me they wanted to give me a $1000 or ever heard of it before. I said I will bring him to the office, and you can offer it to him yourself.

I brought him in the room and told him the compliments the customer had given about him and that I took the liberty to tell them your story. I said they were so moved by your story, so impressed by the sales experience, and liked you so much they want to help you continue by giving you a $1000 to help get your wardrobe started. The old salesman was so moved by their offer he teared up as he responded. "That is the kindest thing anyone has ever offered to do for me. Thank you so much. You are great folks. But I just can't accept it."

He went on to say that getting sober and staying sober has made him reach deep down inside himself. I have been in constant prayer asking God if I deserved a good life after all the bad, I have done. The hardest part has been facing up to, admitting and living with myself for all the hurt I brought on the people that loved me the most. It has been almost unbearable at times. "I truly understand One Day at a Time" He went on to say that it would be easier if he could instantly look more presentable, but as crazy as it sounds looking this way has forced me to go to new heights to show character knowing what people must be thinking of me. But I need that courage, that strength to handle it because that is what will keep me sober. Being allowed to earn my way back to a good job was enough to help, I need to do the rest myself.

That meeting had to be God sending me a message. Let me tell you I was not the only one moved by this man's determination, both customers were in tears. The customer told him if he decided the money could help all he had to do was call.

After the customer had left, I was bothered by the negative comments from my staff. One salesman said since you want to help this old drunk why don't you buy him a pack of cigarettes so he will quit bumming mine. I would have gotten mad normally about their negativity, but I was caught up in what I had witnessed the last couple of hours. I went across the street and bought a pack of cigarettes and gave them to the old salesman making up a story about somebody left them in a car. I told him not to bum any more cigarettes from any of the other salesmen.

I was still concerned that a phone call was going to come from the owner about him and I wondered what I was going to say. How could I make the situation better?

Later that day I did my usual once a week order of Chinese food delivered from Papa Chows. When the food arrived, I discovered I had lost my gold money clip with $630 in it. The delivery guy knew me so I told him I would bring money by later with an extra tip for him.
After I ate quickly, then I walked all over the lot where I had been but did not find it. The clip was a special gift from somebody, I would let the finder keep the cash for the money clip back. I had no sooner walked back into the showroom and sat down when the old salesman walked in and said he just found something out on the lot did anybody lose anything? I said yes, I did. He said can you be more specific? I said a gold money clip with $630 cash in it, 6 100-dollar bills, and 3 10-dollar bills. He said that is it and handed it to me.

I said thanks, then went and sat down in my office wondering if I would have been that honest under the same situation. I wanted to believe I would but, no money, no gas, no cigarettes, and probably very little food. I said a prayer then about 30 seconds later I called him to my office saying I needed him to run an errand for me. I took the $30 out of the clip and told him to take this to the Chinese restaurant and pay for my delivery and tell them to give the change to the delivery fellow. Then I handed him $100 bill and said go buy you a carton of cigarettes and keep that change for gas or food until payday. He said I cannot accept a reward, I said shut up I am not through with the directions for you. I handed him the other $500 and said go to Dillard's in the Mall and spend every penny of this on slacks shirts and a pair of shoes. They have the Sansabelt Wool Slacks on sale I know I just bought two pairs. This is not an offer it is an order I am giving you and I will fire you if you do not do as I say. One more thing do not blow two years of sobriety or it is all over as fast as it started, got it. He said ok if that is what you want boss. I said absolutely and handed him the keys to my demo.

He had been gone for almost 3 hours and I was getting nervous when I heard the owner page me to his office. I knew what this was going to be about. When I got to his office he asked "Johnny Mack, do I have an old drunk bum selling used cars for me now" The description almost made me mad so I said "that doesn't fit the description of anyone I have got working for me" He said don't be coy Johnny Mack what is going on, why all the gossip I'm hearing" Those words no sooner left his mouth when I heard a page from the old salesman to call my office. I did and when he answered I heard him say with lots of enthusiasm "I did exactly as you instructed and stopped by my place to change clothes and God it feels great, thanks boss, you're a good man" I said can you come up to the owner's office right now. He asks if there was a problem and I said not at all.

He arrived looking like a completely different person, a remarkable transformation in appearance. I introduced them and we had a very upbeat visit lasting about 15 minutes with my owner saying he was sure they had met years before at a convention.

After he left the owner asked me "why all this talk about him was being a drunk and a bum." I like this guy" The owner told me that it is a great hire, Johnny Mack, now if we can just keep him. Everybody will be chasing after him for managers' jobs.

He called me a few times every year thanking me and telling me he was still sober. I got a call from him in 2018 telling me he was retiring and thanking me for hiring him 20 years ago.

He said there are two days in his life he will always remember. The day he gave his life to God and became sober and the same date two years later that I hired him.

This is also my favorite true story that happened to me in over 35 plus years in the Automobile Business.

Made in the USA
Columbia, SC
25 July 2024